I CAN DO IT!

I CAN USE THE TELEPHONE

by Susan Ashley

Photographs by Gregg Andersen

Reading consultant: Susan Nations, M.Ed., author/literacy coach/consultant

WEEKLY WR READER
EARLY LEARNING LIBRARY

Please visit our web site at: www.earlyliteracy.cc
For a free color catalog describing Weekly Reader® Early Learning Library's
list of high-quality books, call 1-877-445-5824 (USA) or 1-800-387-3178 (Canada).
Weekly Reader® Early Learning Library's fax: (414) 336-0164.

Library of Congress Cataloging-in-Publication Data

Ashley, Susan.
    I can use the telephone / by Susan Ashley.
       p. cm. — (I can do it!)
    Includes bibliographical references and index.
    ISBN 0-8368-4327-4 (lib. bdg.)
    ISBN 0-8368-4334-7 (softcover)
    1. Telephone etiquette—Juvenile literature. I. Title. II. I can do it! (Milwaukee, Wis.)
  BJ2195.A74   2004
  395.5'9—dc22
                                                     2004045131

This edition first published in 2005 by
Weekly Reader® Early Learning Library
330 West Olive Street, Suite 100
Milwaukee, WI 53212 USA

Copyright © 2005 by Weekly Reader® Early Learning Library

Editor: JoAnn Early Macken
Graphic Designer: Melissa Valuch
Art Director: Tammy West
Picture Researcher: Diane Laska-Swanke
Photographer: Gregg Andersen

Printed in the United States of America

1 2 3 4 5 6 7 8 9 08 07 06 05 04

Note to Educators and Parents

Reading is such an exciting adventure for young children! They are beginning to integrate their oral language skills with written language. To encourage children along the path to early literacy, books must be colorful, engaging, and interesting; they should invite the young reader to explore both the print and the pictures.

I Can Do It! is a new series designed to help young readers learn how ordinary children reach everyday goals. Each book describes a different task that any child can be proud to accomplish.

Each book is specially designed to support the young reader in the reading process. The familiar topics are appealing to young children and invite them to read — and re-read — again and again. The full-color photographs and enhanced text further support the student during the reading process.

In addition to serving as wonderful picture books in schools, libraries, homes, and other places where children learn to love reading, these books are specifically intended to be read within an instructional guided reading group. This small group setting allows beginning readers to work with a fluent adult model as they make meaning from the text. After children develop fluency with the text and content, the book can be read independently. Children and adults alike will find these books supportive, engaging, and fun!

— Susan Nations, M.Ed., author, literacy coach, and consultant in literacy development

I can use the telephone. I can call my friend.

I ask to use the phone. I make sure I know the phone number.

Numbers are listed
in the phone book.
My brother helps me
find the number.

I call my friend.
I press a button
for each number.

I hear a ringing sound. Someone says, "Hello."

I say, "Hello." I give my name. I ask to talk to my friend.

When we are
done talking, I say,
"Good-bye." I hang
up the phone.

The phone helps in an emergency. My parents can call 911.

Emergency

911

Doctor 385-6322
Dad   385-7764
Mom   247-8989

19

My parents answer the telephone when it rings. Is the call for me? Yes!

Glossary

emergency — a sudden and dangerous situation

phone book — a book with a list of phone numbers

press — to push down

For More Information

Books

Alexander Graham Bell. Greg Linder (Bridgestone)

I Wonder Why the Telephone Rings and Other Questions About Communication. Richard Mead (Kingfisher)

Telephones. Joanne Mattern (Enslow)

Telephones. Darlene R. Stille (Compass Point Books)

Web Sites

Cyber Telephone Museum

www.museumphones.com/index2.html
Photos and descriptions of old telephones

Index

About the Author

Susan Ashley has written more than twenty-five books for children. She has lived all over the United States and in Europe. Thanks to her travels, she has become very good at reading maps and writing letters. She also likes making — and eating — sandwiches. Susan lives in Wisconsin with her husband and two cats. The cats like it when she makes tuna sandwiches!